Ups and Downs and In Between

Gaye Louise Trumley

Gaye Louise Creative Writings

www.crowecreations.ca

Ups and Downs and In Between © 2019, Gaye Louise Trumley

GLCW
Gaye Louise Creative Writings

First Crowe Creations Publication September 2019

Cover photo © iStock photo ID:537818932; Credit: sapozhnik
Cover Design © 2019 Crowe Creations
Interior design by Crowe Creations
Text set in Basic Sans SF; headings in Belfast SF

Crowe Creations
ISBN: 978-1-927058-57-2

To All My Angels

Author's Foreword

We all have journeys. They are as mystical as the stars, the moon, the sun, and our planet, Earth. Each journey is different. My poems reflect part of mine. They are created out of feelings and observations. I hope you will enjoy them and think of the journey you have been taking.

Table of Contents

"Life Is a Highway." — Tom Cochrane, from his 1991 album *Mad Mad World*.

My Messages

The shadow envelops me in its black robe.
It bellows words of family that shake my very core.
I stare at my feet which just barely touch the grey floor.
I try not to spoil my dress as I search for a Kleenex in my
    new Easter purse.
Tears stream down my face as my little soul searches for
    answers.
My earthly father turns ever so slowly and stares at my tears
    and asks: "Why are you crying?"
I stop abruptly.
Only to discover the answer many years later.

Laughter in the Blues

It was an ordinary supper.
Spaghetti and meat sauce.
The kitchen was small and we all crowded in.
Silently we ate our food as usual.
We were trained that way.
Then all eyes turned to watch with amazement one of us
    was out of control.
Her spaghetti started to fall off her tray.
Then she smeared it down the sides of her cheeks, like
    misplaced rouge.
Some leftovers hung on her fork and floor.
Her hair began to be coated like a hat.
We stared in horror.
Then, with unspoken silence we burst out with such laughter,
    unrecognizable to each other.
A relief we needed.
The Master was away.

Fountain of Innocence

I combed her soft hair with its little curls that reached to the
top circle of her small, tiny head.
She sat so quietly as if knowing the fingers that touched her
flowed with love.
Her eyes shone as the mirror reflected the transformation.
With an added swirl of colour, I donned a beautiful flower
which brought her to a wide smile as her face glowed
like a June bug's.
Today, I remember and plant that reminder on my own
crown.

Blood Ties

My eyes watch in horror.
The brain cannot connect to the scene in front of me.
Long arms reach the toilet as they secure the young body
    with strength unknown to himself.
The sounds of flushing echo in my ears.
The head comes up; wet at its peaks;
the satanic laugh rings in my ears as a familiar sound.
We carry on as if the hazing was part of life.

The Lighthouse

It wasn't any particular movie.
Just any one.
That was the extent of our communication.
So off we went, not knowing what to expect.
We weren't together very often, so this night was special.
As we bought our popcorn and Coke, it felt like this was our
    way of being close.
The movie began and as it rolled, we became uneasy.
Then more of it made us shake.
As the depth of it showed gruesome slaying of men, women,
    and children, we sank deeper into our chairs.
Finally, eyes half shut and covered, it was over.
We dashed out into the fresh air
    and proclaimed a bond.

Respect

It haunts me.
The time always comes with celebration.
The day one was born.
The day Christ was born.
The day she recalls her position as a mother.
An acknowledgment comes unanswered in the form of a
    card or telephone call.
Her heart rips out in pieces and she half denies her very
    self existence.
I see her eyes and I feel her pain.
It will haunt me over and over till the end of time.

Beyond Existence

Sweet smell
    like something one only senses with innocence.
The breathing is so light I wonder if it is alive
    resting on my shoulder. It feels as if there will be no
    departure.
Will I let it go so easily? Or will I cling to that purity of
    rapture forever in my mind?

Tears of Life

The tears flow with the parting.
They will never end.
We feel each other like two souls who will be forever
    bonded.
Our lives go on, each searching our own single destiny,
    wondering if the tears will ever blend
    with the blood we share.

A Force Greater than Oneself

It was such a little thing
    no one would suspect its control.
Something ate away at my patience,
    started to suck each feeling from me.
I was unaware of its power.
It focused on me.
Then, without warning, my being was taken over.
I grasped for air.
My blood burned with a fever I never knew.
The fear of losing to it was so powerful, I had to escape into
    my being and away from others.
Rage overtook me.
Never did I think this thing called "anger" could be
    so evil.

The Change

I feel dead inside.
Dead, like maggots have fed on every part of my flesh and
    soul.
My nerves tingle on the very edge.
The edge is like the end of reality and the beginning
    of unreality.
Where do I cross over?
When do I cross over?
How do I cross over?
Deep inside I say it will pass.
But will it?

Every "Body" Wants Its "Bond"

My feet rush under me, ever so swift.
My eyes tear up under my dark huge sunglasses.
Must run, run, run.
My sense of where to overtakes me.
My body sits for a time on a bench.
Tears flow harsher than the fountain near.
Is someone looking?
My mind says I can't go home.
My soul is broken.
Must run, run, run.
I spot a pay phone.
He's there and I am saved.

Family

I asked who called.
The name stuns me.
My feelings grip with deep anger, loss and betrayal.
There is nothing more to say, nothing I want to do.
How can years of unfinished business ever be right
   again?
Will they not go away?
Can they not leave me alone?
My heart searches for present healing.
I pray they understand and go their separate ways.

Scattered Thoughts

I look at the green fresh leaves from my window.
I hear the chatter of the television in front of me.
I think of my husband at his uncle's funeral.
I think of my mother, our Chinese food, and her faucets
    to be fixed.
I feel lost in a life of decisions.

Unexpected Surprises

I walk with an energy that urges my legs to go faster.
There are unfamiliar scenes as I pass each corner.
A shop beckons me in where
    I scan the items fruitlessly then hasten out.
I walk again with energy.
I stop at a gleam of light by the road.
Slowly, I pick up the colourful stone.
As I pick it up, my eyes look to see if someone
    watches.
Into my bag it goes, ever so swiftly.
I walk with enthusiasm and think of the wonder of
    the day's events

Choices

The donut drips from his small mouth as he watches.
I carefully feel each toy and examine it.
He won't look into my eyes as I point to my pick on
    the table.
My choice was good.
It was not one of his favourites.
I pass my change into his small hand.
He turns to his father with pride and relief.

Angels

My depression lingers over fear and uncertainty.
Once again, I feel the resentment and frustration
    which, at times, is unbearable.
My eyes close and I hide ever so deep within the
    blankets.
Then, as my mind slips, it acknowledges outside feelings, and
    I hear applause
    applause so faint from the outside.
It feels good.
The applause gets louder, deafening my wounds.
They know.
Each loud clap understands.
I feel their soft touch near my face.
Once again, God has spoken to me through his
    creations.
My soul is again replenished with peace and
    self-esteem.

Untitled

I watch out my kitchen window.
I see her sitting quietly in the sunlight.
The garage doors seem to surround her
    as if protecting her frail body and soul.
Boxes are around her. With each gentle hand,
    which I've come to know for so long,
    she picks up the saved item as if it were her
    precious child;
    her cherished moment; her far-off home.
She ponders over it and looks up to the sky,
    and thinks of times gone.
Many moves; many thoughts; some of pain;
    some of joy, and times that will never be again.
She looks up.
She sees me.
My lifeline.
My beautiful mother.

Printed in *Sparkles in the Sand*,
The National Library of Poetry, 1995

Conquered

His sway is like a strong gladiator's.
Each leg thick and solid.
Each arm ready to lift a thousand swords.
Then with a flash, the guardian swiftly plunges
    the small body into the water with a dumping motion.
Quickly back on solid ground and in his armour of Huggies,
    he gathers his thoughts.
His mouth smiles in delight at his audience.
His voice squeals with victory.
Arms fly up for more, more, more.
And around the pool he goes to conquer.
Soul of bravery.

The Cloth

The weekly chores become never ending.
The dust flies.
As the cloth swipes over all the collected items,
    I wonder for what purpose.
My hand reaches quickly for an article.
Time is precious, but as you place it
    back to the position where it lays, you stop.
Picking it back up, your fingers feel it.
You note how thick and solid it is.
There are grooves in it, smooth and sure.
The colour is crystal clear with a pretty-shaped goose
    on the bottom.
Memories come pouring in as your mind slips back.
You remember, as a girl, this item packed, unpacked,
    placed, replaced, wiped and rewiped.
Has it been that long?
I take care as I place it down and look onto my
    cloth with respect.

Printed in *Good Times Magazine*, September, 1998

Silent Acceptance

My nerves are frazzled.
By circumstances unknown, we meet.
As we chit-chat we decide to have tea or whatever
    at a local restaurant.
She flutters at what to have.
We share a dish.
Our conversation leads to past pictures and
    intimacies too painful to talk about.
It's her day.
She asks "Have I done something wrong?"
No, I reply. We pay the bill.
She gracefully puts her jacket on and whips out
    a new hat.
As if by magic, the hat transforms her. She glows with
    its purchase.
My eyes soften and tell her she looks great.
We part.
Each lifted with our own secret of love.

After the Ashes

They scream with terror as the first smell of smoke comes
    to their nostrils.
Each hangs on to one another.
Their voices shrill so loudly, the heavens open up
    as they burn.
Fresh grey ashes are left in a mound where
    they are blown lightly with the wind and
    scattered through the air.
Then, years later, each flake falls ever so gently.
They are separate, yet one.
Cool, clear and soft.
They make their presence known.
Clean, sparkling, and white, they lay like jewels to cover
    the earth in peace each turn of a new
    winter season.

Needs

Off in the distance I hear the score.
The sound of constant reply is heard as well.
Supper is prepared with enthusiasm
    and romance.
After, we slither into our safe corners of the world,
    deep within our covers.

Legs

Legs hang over the side as the body lies flat on the
      grass, drinking in the sun on the dry face,
      bones so familiar to me by their shape and
      the hand clutching lightly around his bottle.
But how can that be?
I remember those legs.
I remember that bottle.
And I walk by with a tingle in my spine that will never
      be erased from my memory.

Plenty

Perched on top of the canopy he is king.
Here he is free.
Here he is superior to his masters.
Food and air are more plentiful than most of his
      counterparts in the world have.
His huge ego searches for the next catch.
Down he swoops and takes more than he can handle
      off a plate unfinished.
As he makes his getaway across the pool, his daily
      take drops.
Oh well, he says, pickings will be riper later.
Then he flees off with a superior manner, knowing
      he can eat well in his land forever.

Hope

Her hair is white
    her face determined.
She carries buckets of water up the street, over and over.
The procedure goes on and on throughout the day.
The heat scorches her face and arms.
She has a purpose.
The flowers need to be watered.
Besides, she also knows her son lives there.

On a Mission

Her legs are like sticks shoved into huge, black,
    rubber boots.
She owns only the one pair.
Her frail back carries the pack of school books pulling
    her aching shoulders back.
She carries her only worldly possessions in it.
Her massive umbrella hovers to cover
    parts of the tiny body still exposed.
Her hair hangs down the strained face, wet and
    cold against her cheeks.
Body shivering, she pushes by with
    a heavy heart and steers toward
    the mission set out for her that day.

Weekends

He doesn't have to go to battle.
He rests, re-grasps his energy depleted by the week's
    pressures of
    human demands.
As he awakens, it feels good to
    shut out the world.
Silence.
Time is nonexistent.
He is refreshed and the days toll on with
    personal chores of satisfaction.
Nourishment comes with an intimate meal of
    candles and wine.
Dawn arrives and once again begins
    the battle of
    the week that follows.

Friend

We chatter.
Each reveals parts of our self.
It's hard.
Years of chatter, years of trust.
We share those times of
    learning about ourselves, hoping not to
    lose what we began with
    so long ago.

A Taste of New

The carriage is filled with new and exciting items.
It's the focal point of their visit.
The youngest runs and searches each store for
    new adventures.
The middle child's long black hair, like coal, hangs behind
    her head, as her tiny face with
    dancing eyes runs to the carriage for
    the treats.
The eldest sits with her pretty new dress.
She scans the area to find
    a friendly face, so she can fit in
    to this new world.
They all know, so far, this world
    is delicious.

RR

She babbles on as we have other times
    long ago.
This time I feel
    lost and not understood.
As I search my heart for a deeper meaning to my soul,
    words from her touch a core.
Unknown to her,
    we've evolved to a higher spiritual level.

The Prey

I peer the way it peers
    watching The Prey.
We stalk The Prey as it goes from
    one end of the lawn to
    the other.
Slowly our eyes follow,
    watching the moves of The Prey.
She moves her body and eyes slowly.
I move my body and eyes slowly.

Who owns this Prey?

The Prey? My husband finishes and folds
    his watering hose for the evening.

Untitled

My head pounds like a million jackhammers are
    trying to get out.
I visualize the blade on the guillotine coming down and
    giving me release.
The events of the day, and of memories past, seem to be
    fighting against my very sanity.
The telephone rings.
I can't lift myself from the bed.
I am told it is she and she wishes to speak to me.
A message is taken and I try to call back but
    her line is busy.
She has just lost her son to AIDS.

The Guardians

They stand, legs apart, guarding their den.
The dog scurries around using up excess energy.
Their coffee warms their hands and they whisper
    secrets to each other,
    each knowing they protect their precious loved ones
    safe and sound inside
    their castles.

The Visit

Feverishly, we exchange events that have
    passed in the months that made a year.
Each person wanting to be understood.
Each person wanting to be respected.
Each person wanting to be themselves.
Each person wanting to be heard.
Each person wanting to be accepted.
They leave.
Each person feeling loved.

Printed in *The Vine*, June, 1997

Boundary

You are you and
    I am me.
Come together in ecstasy.
Communicate and we'll be one.
You will be you and
    I will be me.

The Bride

She sits calmly as if a trance has captured her.
She eats slowly, like one more piece would
    take the magic away.
People stare at her in total captivation.
The dress sparkles with each pearl and lacy stitch,
    it shines with every move.
A headpiece wraps her neatly done hair and from it
    hangs a flowing veil.
Her guests confess what a day this is.
She opens each card and reads it with
    a depth of understanding far beyond her years.
The gifts are opened with delicate care and
    shown to friends with excitement.
Her shoes pinch her toes and the dress begins to scratch
    her skin from the long day.
Finally, the day is over and she knows it's time to change.
Change into what? she wonders.
The journey God has given her with the First Communion.

The Rope

It's long and thick
    with strong texture.
A proud rope as it holds the bounty.
The bounty clings tightly to it.
Each a cargo ever so precious.
One cargo shakes, slides, twists and turns
    wondering where it will go.
But they all cling hard to the rope because they know
    one slip from it and they
    will be lost before they are found.
Each cargo carries its own precious colours of the world.
None knows its destination as it goes.
Each is fresh and clean, with eyes that shine of the moon
    and the stars.
Oh, rope. Be careful. Watch your cargo
    made from heaven, because
    your hands, they shape our destiny.

Escape

A gust of wind sweeps behind to trap me in.
The voices greet me warmly.
    Like family.
I'm ushered to the famous chair.
Time stands still.
They talk with passion.
They work with passion as
    hair, nails, and toes
    come alive.
Then quietly,
    a gust of wind sweeps me out once more to
    the open world.

Seasons of My Tree

Winter rips through my tree so severely, her branches
    have hardly enough strength to continue.
Rain pelts down so harshly, my tree is exhausted from
    fighting for her permanent position.
Warm air comes again to take
    cold drops from the twigs.
Punishment continues with rain so cold the very
    heart of her wants to snap in two.
Then, as the yellow-crimson, radiant sun begins to fall
    between the houses, a miracle:
With branches reaching for the sky, my tree's soul shines
    magnificently with
    rain drops frozen in time,
    each drop sparkling like a diamond.
Its creator smiles at the beauty unfolding in
    the midst of such torment.

Printed in *Image* magazine, May/June, 1997

Light

The candle flickers as the eye reflects only the
    present.
I find myself enveloped and consumed in it.
Does it seek the deep feelings of others? Or is it
    engulfed with only the flame within.
Surrender to the state of the golden glow, or search for
    meaning through the reflection of others?
Only the candle knows for sure.

Outside — Inside

I step out of the warm water that surrounded me with
 peace.
The soap has cleansed me with its sweet smell of Ivory.
The towel engulfs me so I can hide and feel safe.
I sway to the big open chair to
 my comfort zone.
I was told not to go outside
 that it was not safe.
My friend who holds me close to his bosom whispers:
"Do not be afraid." I will always be inside you.

All in a Day's Work

This house is driving me crazy.
I dress with energy,
    more energy than usual.
The two little ones feel the excitement,
    are still and quiet.
The door snaps back and we gaze at our friend on
    four legs
    who desperately wants to join us.
Down to the park we go on our mission, as if
    we are ants making a new colony.
I speak to one of my workers who comes back for
    tea and to rest as we discuss our world.
Seven wander home, realizing that bonding
    will make better the empire we are building.

Dreams

We are warm and safe.
The sheets smell of Tide and the comforter of Downy.
Our pillows are soft with feathers that sometimes peek through
the case to tickle our noses.
As each night falls, we encase ourselves in these
cocoons to form dreams in our minds of
faraway places.
Then, as daybreak emerges, we listen to the pitter-patter of
feet touching the floor and wonder
who will emerge as
the beautiful butterfly today.

Spring Is Green and Dances

It dances with each soft gentle wind through
    its leaves.
It dances with each blade of grass applauding the
    cool breeze.
It dances off the tops of budding bushes as they
    reach up to steal the radiant sun.
It dances to the wavering stems on crimson
    tulips as they search for their very source
    of existence.
It dances to the green leaves that dazzle your eyes
    for the first time through the soft wind.
Now do you see the green spring as it dances?

Printed in *Shelter from the Storm*, Poetry Guild, 1998

About the Author

Gaye Louise Trumley was born in Toronto, Ontario, in 1946. Her parents, Lt. Col. Richard Trumley and Ruth Pearce Trumley, dedicated their lives to the Royal Canadian Air Force.

Gaye Louise had the opportunity to travel extensively, as far as the United States, Canada, and Europe, where she learned to adjust to the life of a "nomad". Gaye Louise is the second of five siblings. Ending up in Ottawa in 1970, she worked for the Federal Government for twenty-seven years. She also had a working experience with the Bank of Nova Scotia and the Royal Canadian Air Force. In 1977, Gaye Louise married Frank Dennis Parisotto who is originally from Sudbury, Ontario.

Gaye Louise is the author of *Forces in the Air*: *An Autobiography of a Canadian Forces Brat*, 2010, Crowe Creations, as a tribute to her mother. Gaye Louise plans a non-fiction book to continue her new talents under "Gaye Louise Creative Writings".

Gaye Louise enjoys aerobics, yoga, walking, compiling picture albums for family and friends, and dining out.